ABOUT THE AUTHOR: Mollee Kruger's five volumes of light poetry display a technical wizardry that hauls out the human condition and gives it a good swift kick. Editor and playwright as well as author of a weekly newspaper column of topical verse, which ran nationally for twenty years in ethnic publications, she has received countless awards for serious and light verse. Her commemorative book *Yankee Shoes* was honored by the American Revolution Bicentennial Administration in 1976. She wrote a musical production celebrating the 350th birthday of Maryland, created Bicentennial Minutes marking the 200th anniversary of the U.S. Constitution and belongs to the National League of American Pen Women.

ABOUT THE ARTIST: Yolanda Frederikse, watercolorist and printmaker, exhibits her work nationally and in the Washington, D.C. area, where she is affiliated with several leading galleries. Winner of a National Endowment for the Humanities Fellowship in 1975 and many awards over the years, she is a Signature Member of the National Watercolor Society and a Maryland State President of the National League of American Pen Women. In 1975 her work was selected for reproduction by the American Bicentennial Commission. She is listed in *American Artists, An Illustrated Survey of Leading Contemporaries, 1990.* Her work underscores boldly the excitement, bravado, and ultimate heartbreak in the life of Columbus.

Comments on Mollee Kruger's books:...."Should be on the nightstand until it's read from cover to cover"___ Sherri L. Rice, librarian...."Has dealt with serious material in a meaningful and light-hearted style..what a delight to read Mollee Kruger's poetry" ___Julie Frank Pick, broadcaster...*Yankee Shoes* is to be remembered as a "special" of our time..as John Warner is doing, the book is to be an important part of the archives of the Maryland Bicentennial"___ Louise Gore, Bicentennial Commission chair..."Very talented"___Baltimore Evening Sun..." you'll wish to re-read, share with people you like..."___ Hannah Grad Goodman

Other Books by Mollee Kruger

A COMPLETE GUIDE FOR THE COLLEGE GIRL, 1968

UNHOLY WRIT, 1970*

MORE UNHOLY WRIT, 1973*

YANKEE SHOES, 1975*

DAUGHTERS OF CHUTZPAH, 1983*

* These books can be ordered from

Maryben Books
P.O. Box 1293
Rockville, Maryland 20849-1293

The poem "Brotherly Breach" was awarded first prize in the 1988 Alice Sherry Memorial contest sponsored by the Poetry Society of Virginia

ADMIRAL OF THE MOSQUITOES

Mollee Kruger

Illustrated by Yolanda Frederikse

A MARYBEN BOOK

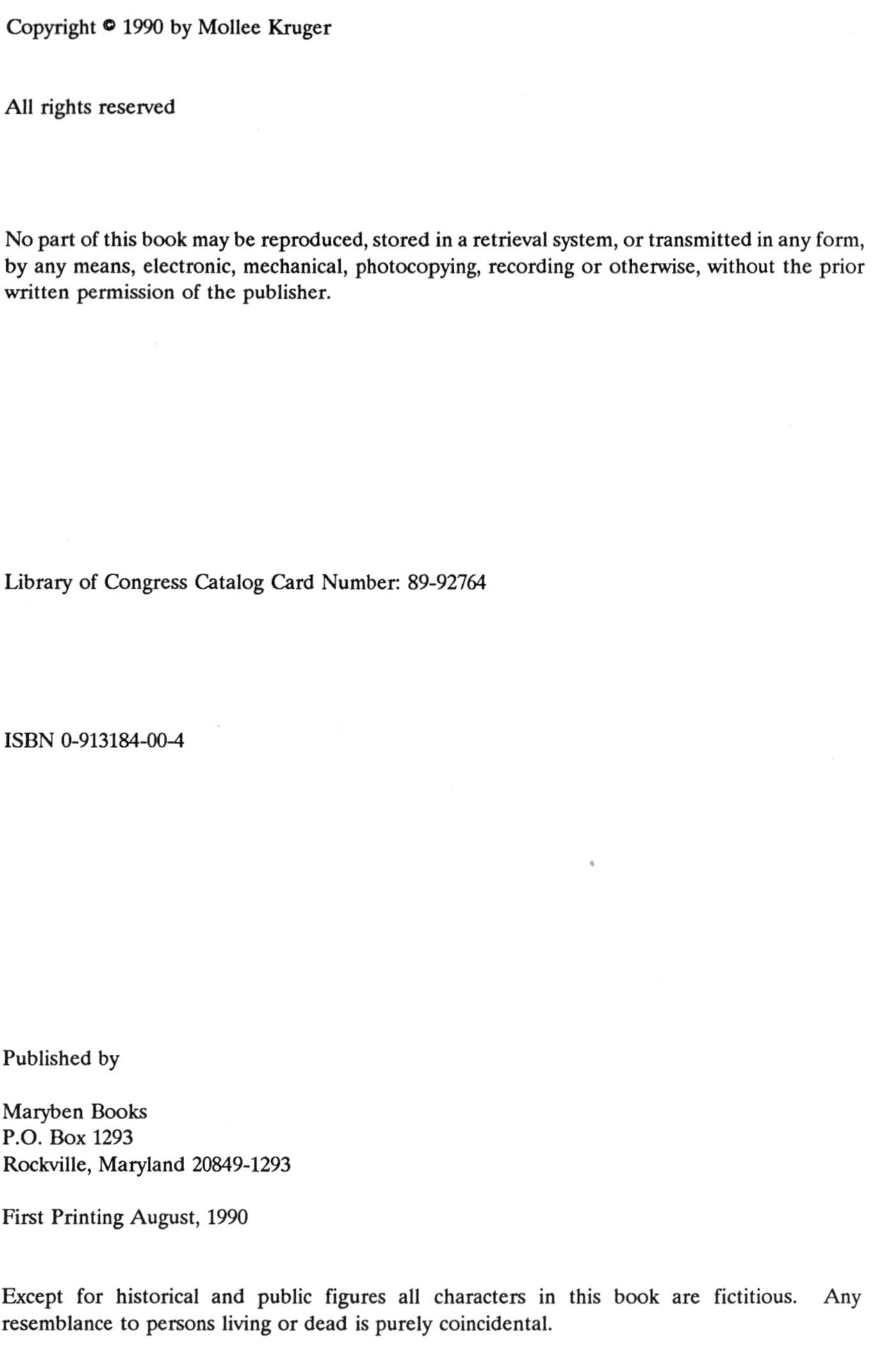

Library of Congress Catalog Card Number: 89-92764

ISBN 0-913184-00-4

Published by

Maryben Books
P.O. Box 1293
Rockville, Maryland 20849-1293

First Printing August, 1990

Dedication

Because the State of Maryland has always been a haven for the seafaring stranger, this book is dedicated to Lord Baltimore's unique colony founded one hundred and forty-two years after the first landing of Columbus in the New World.

In addition to the Free State's people of diverse ethnic backgrounds and politics -- Democrats, Republicans, Independents -- this labor of love is dedicated to the outstanding multicultural state leaders of the 1990's and the proud cultures that molded them:

> to the industrious German-American neighborhood that produced Governor William Donald Schaefer, who will be remembered as a modern Columbus, sailing where the faint of heart fear to go
>
> to the classical Greek heritage of Senator Paul Sarbanes, a descendant of the civilization that gave the world democracy and inspired Columbus, the Renaissance man
>
> to the artistic and freedom loving Polish origins of Senator Barbara Mikulski, like Columbus, a trailblazer, Maryland's first woman to represent the state in the United States Senate

And we further dedicate these pages to two others who represent ingredients vital to our story: to the glorious traditions found in the Italian roots of Constance Morella, United States House of Representatives, Shakespearean scholar and author of our Foreword; and to the Hispanic inspiration and friendship of Dr. Alicia Juerro Roqué, philosopher, educator, and Cuban-born direct descendant of the Spanish explorer Ponce de León.

The author, a native Marylander and herself the child of immigrants, also salutes the future. May you look back at us and know that cultural diversity has been America's greatest strength. We are every one of us a child of Columbus.

Preface

Publication is the garage sale of the mind, thank you, Emily Dickinson, and I have chosen to empty into the reader's perceptions a folio of frenzied India-inked Krazy Kats conjured up half a millennium away from Columbus and his time. Light verse is the only way I can deal with a near mythical figure, the Admiral of the Mosquitoes. That's what they called him. In the section "The Entropy of Success" you'll see that after the first journey of discovery, it was downhill all the way for him.

A folk poet-light versifier the likes of me is also an admiral of mosquitoes. In addition to four volumes of light poetry, I have written and published over 1500 topical and religious poems in a weekly newspaper column for twenty years. For most of my life I have directed lightwinged stinging swarms of rhyme and meter at the passing reader. But now for the first time I tell an ancient tale that encompasses present and future.

The Columbus story most of us know consists of the date 1492; the *Niña*, the *Pinta*, and the *Santa María*; and Ferdinand and Isabella. There's more. And maybe because we first learned about Columbus when we were very young, it seems the right touch to present a story with contemporary insights written in the style of poems remembered from childhood.

Although I began this collection tongue-in-cheek, every now and then poems cropped up that didn't fit the mold. Good, said I, unpredictability is the first rule of history, which also jumps from the trivial to the tragic. What's more, along the way the voice of an irate Columbus arose, resenting my banter and throwing the words back into my face. To keep him happy I allowed him his say, but for the most part he steered clear of the light stuff and insisted instead on a kind of biblical cadence. Or at least that's what I heard when I held the sea shell up to my ear.

"If you have faith," he wrote in the introduction to his *Book of Prophecies,* which he planned to do in verse but never got around to, "you may be very confident of victory." But he also spoke of a place "where gold is born" and he never really found it. Victory also means resilience and determination. Our country in celebrating the Quincentennary of the Discovery of America would do well to seek that kind of victory. And it doesn't hurt to pay attention to what history and the prophets say to us. Look what they did for Columbus.

The following references are recommended to the reader:
The Log of Christopher Columbus, Robert H. Fuson; *The Story of Don Cristóbal,* Björn Landström; *The Life of the Admiral Christopher Columbus by his son Fernando,* translated by Benjamin Keen; *Christopher Columbus*, Ernle Bradford; *Christopher Columbus*, Gianni Granzotto; *Admiral of the Ocean Sea,* Samuel Eliot Morison; *Sails of Hope*, Simon Wiesenthal; *History of the Indies*, Bartolomé de Las Casas; *Christopher Columbus, Mariner*, Samuel Eliot Morison; *Columbus in the New World*, Bradley Smith; other references: *The Encyclopedia of the Jewish Religion*, edited by R.J. Zwi Werblowsky and Geoffrey Widgoder; *A History of the Jews*, Solomon Grayzel; *A Concise History of Latin American Culture*, Pedro Henríquez Ureña; *The Colonial Heritage of Latin America*, Stanley J. Stein and Barbara H. Stein; *A Report to the Congress by the Christopher Columbus Quincentenary Jubilee Commission, 1987;* Christopher Columbus Family Chapel, pamphlet, Boal Mansion and Museum, Boalsburg, Pa.; "Dim Galaxies Discovered in Distant Void", The Washington Post; "A Small Statue for the 'Pickle Dealer' Who Gave America His Name," Jay Mathews, The Washington Post, Oct. 10, 1988; Book of Esdras, The Apocrypha; Book of Isaiah, The Holy Scriptures.

Thanks also to Congresswoman Constance Morella, United States House of Representatives, Maryland 8th Congressional District; Mickey Reed, aide to Representative Morella; John Gudie, Chairman of the Christopher Columbus Quincentenary Jubilee Commission; Francisco Martinez-Alvarez, Acting Director and William Miner, Program Director of the Christopher Columbus Quincentenary Jubilee Commission and distinguished Commissioners; Governor William Donald Schaefer's Commission on Maryland 1992, Ann D. Hartman, Executive Director; Jennie M. Forehand, Maryland House of Delegates, 17th Legislative District; Dr. Alicia Juarrero Roqué, Prince George's Community College; Madeleine Jacobs, Smithsonian Institution; the Montgomery County Public Library system; the Montgomery County Council, the Montgomery County Commission on the Humanities; Jerome Kruger, the Johns Hopkins University; Len, Joe, and Dina Kruger.

Rockville, Maryland October 3, 1989

Table of Contents

Preface ix
Foreword xi
Brief Chronology xii
Ballad in a Barrel xiii

CARTOON COLUMBUS 2

On Discovered Islands 3
Memo Pad 4
Salesmanship 5
Beatriz de Peraza y Bobadilla 5
Falling Off the Admiral's Log 7
Good Old Days 8
Foreign Entanglements 9
One Good Tern Deserves Another 10
Five Hundred Years of Step-Ins 11
Doggerel 12
The Romance of Martin Alonso Pinzón 13
For Immediate Release 16

PERSONS OF PASSAGE 18

Mothers of Nation 19
Felipa Moniz de Perestrello 20
Beatriz Enriques de Harana 21
Omission 22
The Fourth Ship 23
The Older Sister 24
The Ultimate Weapon 25
The Brother-in-Law 26
Rightful Heirs 27
Amerigo Vespucci 28

HARK! HARK! THE HARQUEBUS! 30

Made In Heaven 31
Fish and Guests Smell After Three Days 32
Who Has the Last Cough Now? 33
Where Gold Is Born 34
Hark! Hark! the Harquebus! 35
Hunters and Gatherers 36
Ignorance 37
Tribes Lost and Found 38

THE ENTROPY OF SUCCESS 40

The Higher Education of Columbus 41
Second Time Around 42
Running It Into the Ground 44
Unlucky Three 45
The Path Downward 46
Governor Bobadilla 47
Bon Voyage and Good Riddance 48
Last Voyage 49
The Great Khan 51
After the Fact 52
Caribbean Mutiny 53

THE BIBLE BUFF 56

Apocryphal Story 57
Prophetic Paths 58
A Political Truth 59
Civil Servants of the Bible 60
Higher Math 61
Unprofitable Prophet 62
Brotherly Breach 63
Connubially Cononical Columbus 64
The Poem He Never Wrote 65

WHERE GOLD IS BORN 68

Humble Origins 69
More Undiscovered Islands 70
The Yarn of the Bunion Acres 71
A 1930-ish Folk Ballad 72
The Statue Speaks Again 75
July 4 76
Thoroughbreds 77
The Visit 79
Another Lady of the Club 80
El Escritorio 81
Dim Galaxies 82
To 2092: Ahoy! 83

Epilogue: Time and America 84

Foreword

Will Rogers once said, "We are all here for a spell, (so) get all the good laughs you can." There are a few things that are "more American" than humor. Our society places a high value on a good sense of humor and on those who can laugh at themselves as well as others.

So what better way to celebrate the quincentennial of the discovery of America than by engaging in a pastime that is quintessentially American: humor? One look at the past literary accomplishments of the gifted author and historian, Mollee Kruger, is evidence enough that her talents are aptly suited to take on the task of bringing Christopher Columbus into our homes and into our hearts--to better understand and appreciate our earliest American heritage. In the tradition of Mark Twain, Will Rogers, and today, Garrison Keillor, Mollee Kruger gives us *Admiral of the Mosquitoes*. Typically, we don't think of Columbus' travels as particularly funny. That is, until we examine them closely as Ms. Kruger did. After all, it *is* amusing that in 1992 what we are celebrating, the 500th anniversary of the discovery of America, is really the celebration of a navigational error committed half a millennium ago. This is not to say that Columbus' discovery of America, however unintentional it may have been, is unworthy of our celebration. But it does point out that his journey to America was both a drama and a comedy just like life itself.

Mollee Kruger's depiction of Columbus' travels is much more than a comic endeavor. Through light verse, Ms. Kruger has managed to convey with remarkable aptitude a sense of the mystique of Columbus in the New World. This volume enables readers, young and old, to replace the drudgery of textbooks with the pleasure of poetry. And what a pleasure it is. How better to describe the creative wizardry of words on the following pages than in the definition that Robert Frost once gave: "A poem begins in delight and ends in wisdom." In *Admiral of the Mosquitoes*, Ms. Kruger places the protagonist, Cristóbal Colón (or Cristoforo, or sometimes just Colombo), in a timeless milieu: between the biblical prophets and contemporary cliches. Abraham and Elijah are juxtaposed with civil servants, whistleblowers, and press releases. We are all part of the continuum.

Constance A. Morella
8th District, Maryland

Congress of the United States
House of Representatives

Brief Chronology

1451	Columbus born in Genoa
1470-78	Goes to sea, becomes a mapmaker
1479	Marries Felipa Moniz de Perestrello, spends time in Porto Santo, Portugal
1480-81	Son Diego born, death of Felipa
1482-86	Voyage plans rejected by Portugese, Spanish dukes, presents plan to Ferdinand and Isabella
1488	Son born to mistress Beatriz Enriques de Harana
1490	Voyage plan rejected in Spain, brother seeks help in England and France without success
1492-93	Moors defeated in Spain; Columbus receives backing of Spanish monarchs; leaves Palos for Indies day after Jews are expelled from Spain; docks at Canary Islands, visits Governor Beatriz de Peraza y Bobadilla; near mutiny on ship, San Salvador sighted, claims land for Spain; *Santa Maria* lost, rivalry with Pinzón brothers, storm hits ships on return home, Columbus throws his records of voyage overboard; Pinzón arrives in Palos few hours after Columbus, who receives highest honors at Court; begins second voyage, finds men left behind at fort massacred by Indians
1494	Founds fort of Isabela, explores Cuba and makes crew sign statement swearing that Cuba is part of the mainland, exploitation of Indians, epidemics, mutinous men, explores Jamaica and adjacent islands, becomes ill, returns to Isabela
1495	Royal Inspector arrives; sends back unfavorable report to Court about conditions in colony
1496	Columbus returns to Spain, humiliated
1497	Stays at Court and hides out in Seville monastery
1498	Begins third voyage, sights Trinidad, sails along coast of South America, claims he has discovered biblical Garden of Eden
1499	Chaos on Española, Columbus fights off mutiny
1500	New royal governor Francisco de Bobadilla arrives to establish law and order; arrests Columbus; returns him to Spain in irons; Ferdinand and Isabella release him and receive him at Court
1502	Begins fourth voyage, visits Martinique and environs, refused permission to enter Santo Domingo harbor by royal governor Nicholás de Ovando; explores coasts and harbors of Central America, illness, near madness
1503-04	Fierce fighting with Indians, further explorations, suppresses mutiny on Española; Columbus and party rescued; goes to Santo Domingo; returns to Spain; Isabella dies
1505-06	Refuses honors and Spanish land in exchange for position of Viceroy of Indies, seeks to negotiate with new queen, madness, dies embittered in Valladolid

Ballad in a Barrel

Consider the plight of Columbus, my readers,
Returning to Spain from his travels,
Prepared to collect on the wonders he found
Until his agenda unravels.

Horrendous, the storm that envelops his passage,
The elements howling and flaying:
His men promise gold for the holiest shrines
If God will pay heed to their praying.

The wind is as wild as a sinner bedeviled,
The sky and the water igniting,
Our Admiral, foiled in his cabin below,
Is frantic to salvage his writing.

He fears that his fame will be vanquished forever,
Erased by a ship that is sinking,
And others will reap from the monarchs of Spain
The credit for all he'd been thinking.

He cradles his journal, the child of his venture,
With oilskin he hastens to bind it,
And placed in a barrel, it's thrown overboard
In hopes that somebody will find it.

A panicky gesture, a lost First Edition,
Destroyed by its nervous creator,
And who brought his tale in a barrel ashore?
Did anyone find the thing later?

Each century voyagers spot it, "Eureka!"
From Greenland to Santo Domingo,
From every location that harbors a beach,
And in every conceivable lingo.

But this is a version not earlier sighted,
Fished out with appropriate timing,
A waterlogged journal five centuries old,
Improved and enlivened with rhyming.

"There go the sons of the
Admiral of the Mosquitoes,
of the man who discovered
the lands of vanity and fraud..."

...catcalls of disillusioned Castilian
ex-colonists in 1500

"What is history but a fable agreed upon?"

...Napoleon Bonaparte

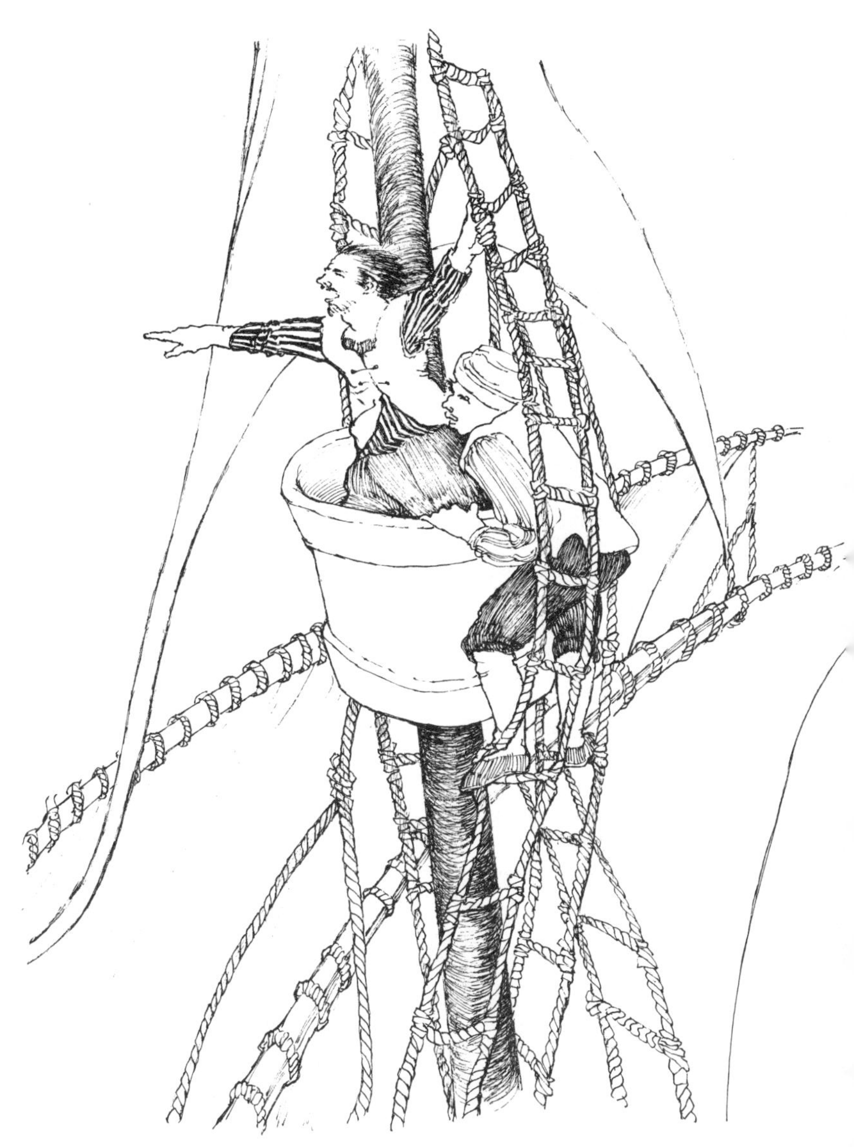

CARTOON COLUMBUS

3

On Discovered Islands

No self-help books were in the stores
designed for Someone Who Explores,
No seminars, no twice-told tales
of how to tilt unbalanced scales,
So granted that he knew his quest
was reaching Asia, sailing west,
where best to push, how strike it rich?
On whom to work the proper pitch?
He beat the bushes seeking backers
(The Portugese believed him crackers)
and when he lobbied Spanish dukes,
they offered wine and mild rebukes
though some, who thought he made good sense,
explained while safely on the fence,
"The private sector can't supply
much flour for pastry in the sky;
the types who keep that kind of cash
are privy to a princely stash.
Forget us small fry in the ranks,
you need Big Bucks from megabanks."
And sure enough, his bid sat well
With Ferdinand and Isabelle.

The message of this tale is clear:
don't grub for peanuts from a peer,
In launching superhuman deals,
it's wise to spin the Biggest Wheels.

Memo Pad

Each day he clutched within his fists
the bills of lading, cargo lists
of means and ends and ports of call,
late visits to the shopping mall,

slick syllables to woo new men
and ink to feed an eager pen,
pale salted beef and yellow cheese
and insights from the Portugese,

enclosed with barrel-brine advice
from royal bureaucrats, and rice,
dried chick peas, arrogance and banners,
Italian flair and Spanish manners,

the wine to mollify his nights
and Scriptures from the Israelites.
He knew the holy text consists
of itemized sequential lists,

an exhortation sketched in stone,
commandments to pursue alone
the asymmetrical design
that contradicts the party line.

Uncatalogued, his longest list
was those who dread an optimist.

5

Salesmanship

What do you promise a Castilian queen?
How do you get her to give you the nod?
You promise a kingdom she never has seen,
A room with a view in the palace of God.

You promise the spread of the Word in her name,
And hand her an Oscar Award-winning role
Of saving the heathen from brimstone and flame,
A gem in the crown to embellish her soul.

(And if, as a codicil, you can insert
Gold, spices, and silver, it hardly can hurt.)

Beatriz de Peraza y Bobadilla

When a man is as driven as Christopher was,
Fanatical, passionate, cranky,
And should he discover the girl of his dreams,
IT's hard to arrange hanky-panky.

He scarcely had sailed from the harbor at dawn
Toward the isles that they call the Canaries,
When the rudder gave out on the ship of Pinzón
Delaying our brave emissaries.

Now governing one of the neighboring isles
Was a woman (a fact that's surprising),
Whose husband, attracted to young native girls,
Was zapped in a minor uprising.

This widow once dazzled the court of Seville,
The Queen found the maid disconcerting,
And she married her off to an overseas spouse
To terminate Ferdinand's flirting.

6

Columbus thought maybe the beauty would help
With suitable vessels to lend him,
And who knew what pleasure erotic and wild,
His hostess would care to extend him?

He twiddled his thumbs for twelve maddening days
Till the lady returned from vacation,
While Pinzón rigged the *Pinta* up better than new
And the trip languished under sedation.

The charmer arrived, "Let the good times begin!"
She ordered, this Venus of ladies,
Columbus, bewitched, could have gathered his men
And told them to buzz off to Hades.

And yet at her table, he heard lavish tales
Of land sighted west in the ocean,
A clear invitation he couldn't resist,
(He stifled his school-boy devotion.)

He might have remained there, entwined in her arms,
A gubernatorial stand-in,
But prophecy beckoned like wind from the sea,
The destiny he had his hand in.

And what if he'd given it up for his love,
And married his well-to-do madam?
He might have been happier combing the beach,
But no one would know him from Adam.

7

Falling Off the Admiral's Log

His crew was nasty from the start,
And sneered behind his back,
They gossiped, "This outlandish mind
Has bounded off the track."

He kept two logs to mix them up,
And when they would complain,
"We're closer than you think," he lied,
"Though scarcely out of Spain."

From time to time the sailors cheered
In error shouting, "Land!"
Yet in his heart he knew they'd sailed
Much farther than he planned.

The early bird, he swore, who spotted
Land would be imbursed,
Though back home in Castile he knew
He'd claim he saw it first.

They sighted the Bahamas, where
Each seaman got a tan,
And craned their necks for sushi bars,
Which island was Japan?

Was Cuba not Cipanu land?
"These isles," he wrote, "confound us,"
(Today he wouldn't search for long:
Japan is all around us.)

8

Good Old Days

Now the *Santa María* was hardly great shakes,
The ship wasn't one of your higher priced makes;
Our culprit was Palos, a sea-faring town,
Which ruffled some feathers and angered the Crown.
Instead of the monarchs decreeing them killed,
The penalty was that the township be billed
For launching Columbus the following year,
Supplying the ships he could sail from their pier.

The *Santa María* was wrong for the course,
He eyed the broad beam of the clumsy gift horse,
And spent his whole voyage immersed in lament,
Deploring this scow that his fortunes had sent.
"Our warranty doesn't hold water," he railed,
"At least not so much as what has to be bailed,
Those malcontent villagers opted to fudge,
One's sure to cut corners when bearing a grudge."

The Admiral sighed to his cabin boy, "Kid,
They could have done better by me than they did;
I wanted a caravel, top-of-the-line,
This klutz of a ship I'm ashamed to call mine."
The townsmen of Palos felt little concern,
Who ever expected those clods would return?
The *Santa María* was nothing to lose,
A throw-away ship for a lunatic's cruise.

The sharpies of Palos had tossed him a bone,
But weren't going to offer their best as a loan,
And crossing the ocean, he quaked in his bunk,
(Three months after landing the lemon had sunk.)

9

Foreign Entanglements

The gulfweed is a pesky plant
akin to our hydrilla
that houses riverbeds and bay
within a tangled villa.

And warily the men on board
the New World's first armada
beheld the kelp with crieds of "Help!"
which generated *nada.*

They feared becoming tangled in
a net of dense sargassos
and dreaded that they'd spend their days
trussed up in algae lassos.

We poets paddling for our words
must risk the same propensity:
it's easy to be strangled in
a Mare Sargassum density.

One Good Tern Deserves Another

The nearer to the land they sailed,
The more the angry seamen railed,

The more the signs were manifest
That spelled an ending to their quest,

The flock of seabirds (petrels, terns),
The frigate birds, the floating ferns,

The more of hope, the more they roared,
"Let's pitch Columbus overboard!"

The devil take the damned Bahamas,
Who knew when next they'd see their mamas?

In every century each hour
The helpless seek a sense of power,

The Common Men, emerging scions
Escaping from the jaws of lions

No longer pleased with empty futures,
Attempt to rip their binding sutures,

And once they've snapped a single fetter,
Or find conditions getting better,

And once the signs point toward the heavens,
They rage at sixes and at sevens

And leery like the doubting Thomas
May lose sight of the lush Bahamas.

11

Five Hundred Years of Step-ins

The Admiral observed at once
a trait he thought un-Spanish,
the torsos waiting on the beach,
both feminine and mannish

were covered by no underwear,
no shoulder strap or button.
The sailors rubbed their eyes and yelled,
"Them folks ain't wearin' nuttin'!"

From weeks at sea, his sweaty crew
was swaddled in a quandary
and wondered when they hit the beach
how best to do their laundry.

But when they chose to dump their wash
on girls with whom they'd flirted,
they found the labor force had fled,
the villages deserted.

And so they scrubbed their skivvies in
the Carib Sea on Mondays;
(Surprising that they didn't call
those islands the West Undies.)

Doggerel

Did Noah quarter on his Ark
the kind of dog that doesn't bark?

You think my query slightly nuts?
The Spanish found them in the huts,
mum flea bags quiet not by choice,
repressed and reticent (no voice).

And though Colombo in his log
reports this clammed up, barkless dog,
some elbow benders in saloons
would call them possums or raccoons.

The natives found these pooches cute
who wagged their tails, but pleaded mute.

Be glad the modern canine barks,
or he'd be useless to the Narcs.

13

The Romance of Martín Alonso Pinzón

Come bellow a ballad
of backbiting greed,
of friendship turned rancid,
ambition's stampede
                    and the partner of Cristoforo

Pinzón was a pilot,
an owner of ships,
who argued at court for
the first of the trips
                    forthright partner of Cristoforo

He haunted the taverns
in search of recruits,
a boon to Columbus
with no Spanish roots
                    useful partner of Cristoforo

Pinzón and his brothers
at neck-breaking pace
pushed forward, insuring
the journey took place
                    seasoned partner of Cristoforo

He planned it for years
and would not let it fizz,
and perhaps the whole concept
was basically his
                    equal partner of Cristoforo

He captained the *Pinta*
from sunrise till dark,
the best of three vessels,
a seaworthy bark
                    salty partner of Cristoforo

14

Committed to danger,
and glory and Spain,
he sensed that Columbus
at best was a pain
chary partner of Cristoforo

A month before landing,
he scored a bad break,
and yodeled, "Land ho!"
in a painful mistake
blushing partner of Cristoforo

Then Pinzón had a hunch
they should alter their course,
but the plan stayed unplayed
though he talked himself hoarse
nagging partner of Cristoforo

When the anchor was dropped,
Pinzón's crowd disappeared
and the *Pinta* sailed off
as the Admiral feared
sneaky partner of Cristoforo

Had he hightailed it home
to stake out his own claim,
and collect all the marbles,
walk off with the game
crafty partner of Cristoforo?

When the *Pinta* returned,
acrimonious flack
and some rash accusations
flew hither and back
wounded partner of Cristoforo

15

There developed a truce:
they would share in the game,
but the tenor of honor
was never the same
                    rueful partner of Cristoforo

So they cast off for Spain,
and Columbus turned pale
when the ships were endangered
in gale after gale
                    dripping partner of Cristoforo

Our good Admiral shook
and expected the worse:
that Pinzón would outwit him
by getting there first
                    speedy partner of Cristoforo

Although Martin Alonso
arrived well ahead,
the royals expected
Columbus instead
                    ignored partner of Cristoforo

Columbus accused him
of devious things
like beating his time in
the presence of kings
                    maligned partner of Cristoforo

The worry was wasted,
Pinzón stepped aside:
five days after landing,
the gentleman died
                    silent partner of Cristoforo

16

For Immediate Release

"On my return from Voyage One,
I knew you can't go far
unless you get the story out:
Castilian PR.

"And so I wrote a letter which
recounted what I found;
I had some copies made and sent
my press release around.

"To merchants, noblemen, and priests
my message was dispatched;
I'd beat the others to the punch
before some plot was hatched

"to rob me of my rightful place,
and shear me of my prize;
The brothers Pinzón and their crew
were double-crossing guys.

"It's said this marked the first time when
a major story broke
that someone with a nose for news
conveyed it to the folk

"And got the message out post haste
with such simplicity,
a coup in mastering the art
of mass publicity.

"Perhaps I overplayed my hand
and carried it too far,
America, inspired by me,
is wired for slick PR."

PERSONS OF PASSAGE

19

Mothers of Nations

A trilogy here of the women he knew,
the ones who were kinder to him than his crew,
the phantoms of females whom Time has forgot
like those who inspired him and garnished his cot,
the faceless obscurities nobody sings,
his wife whom he buried, his mistress sans rings.
First, garlands for her who produced him at birth,
conceiving the genius who conquered the earth.
Let's hear it, you feminists, viola strings
            for Susanna di Fontanorossa

Susanna, his mother, does nobody care
this commoner nurtured her boy with the flair
to pole vault the ocean and startle the stars,
a helmsman of riddles, a regent of tars?
And who was this lady whose son could expound
on theories of distance, a world that was round,
in Latin and three other lingos with ease,
including Castilian and Old Portugese?
Applause, daughters, mothers, an ear-splitting sound
            for Susanna di Fontanorossa

And how did she give him the chutzpah to speak
in castles to nobles and kings at the peak,
and how could he learn about solids and lines,
circumferences, surfaces, biblical signs,
of oceans, peninsulas, continents, isles,
or ways to bedazzle a queen with his smiles
when few of the neighbors' kids read or did sums?
That's all the more reason this accolade comes,
a standing ovation to honor the trials
            of Susanna di Fontanorossa

20

Felipa Moniz de Perestrello

"Seems the first wife died in childbirth,"
        wrote the scholar, nonchalantly,
"or perhaps she died thereafter."
        Does it matter anyway?
Faded tapestry of Mother,
        she was bearer of Diego,
son of Cristovão Colom,
        who secured her heart in Lisbon
and became a Portugese,
        how convenient for the genius.

Born to lesser noble parents,
        bringing more than weaver's dowry,
she was married to her sailor,
        and she waved him off to sea.
It was there in Porto Santo,
        where his woman had connections,
he conceived the turquoise journey,
        and he audited the breeze.
It was there ambition seized him
        when he saw the tidal spittle
of outlandish copper bodies
        never seen with Europe's eyes.

Scholars spend a life-time looking
        for the kindling of Columbus,
capture theories in fat volumes
        like grey herrings in a net,
but Felipa, who propelled him,
        is deemed lucky to have wed him,
and nobody sifts her dust
        on three-by-fives.

Sweet Felipa, keep your vigil
        in your plot of dear nonentity
Beside the dying sea.

21

Beatriz Enriques de Harana

He wouldn't marry her outright,
Perhaps she was too poor,
Too ordinary, too unwashed,
Too tethered to the shore.

Columbus found her in Castile
(He didn't have a pot),
Itinerant, he peddled books,
A fact he soon forgot.

She bore the man a snobbish son,
Fernando, in her prime,
Who pushed away the shabby wharf
To take a courtly climb.

But in his will Columbus begged,
"Make helping her your goal,
I owe her gold for what she gave,
It eats away my soul."

He wouldn't marry her outright
Or share the jeweled compass,
A woman of her time she was,
Who never raised a rumpus.

Omission

We've sung of adversaries' ploys
but bypassed the Columbus boys,
whose sons and brothers interact,
a note the schoolbooks fail to noise.

Fastidious to deal with fact
to which one's siblings can't be tacked,
much simpler to recall one name
than juggle luggage overpacked.

Their relatives don't share acclaim
with those who earn the kiss of fame,
and bloodlines are a dreadful bore
(save Uncle Vanya, Auntie Mame).

Although they're pleasant to ignore,
Colombo boys (and girls) did more
in helping Christopher explore
than they are given credit for.

23

The Fourth Ship

(Note: Sharing the waters with the Nina, Pinta, *and* Santa Maria *before sunrise on August 3, 1492, a last shipload of Spanish Jews waited for the turning tide to carry them away into banishment.)*

What three ships are those, my mother,
Loading for the sea?
Hush my child, they don't concern us,
Or our misery.

It's the Ninth of Ab, my daughter,
Fast of our lament,
On this day the Temple fell,
Jerusalem was spent.

How much longer waiting, mother,
In this airless hold,
Till the wind is blowing southward,
And our birthright sold.

Why must we go roaming, mother,
On a royal whim?
Piety without compassion
Sings a hollow hymn.

Who will take us in, my mother,
Spain is all we know,
Who will welcome homeless people?
Where can exiles go?

Will we find a harbor, mother,
Some protected bay?
Time will comfort mourners, daughter,
God will find a way.

24

The Older Sister

Born in a different town, our Latin sister
when the Spanish motherland had little time for her
born when the mother bent at her silver and gold washboard,
busy, no time to take from squalling demands
of feudal ways, the old European ways
being all the family knew
born undisciplined to the new world,
to grow beneath the captains general
born with all the errors of
distracted parents on her head forever,
the ways set down by necessity
the spikes of expediency, blood and spoils,
she sat back passive, older sister, fat,
soft and sweet as papaya
to wait for her own time to come.

But we popped from the womb, baby upstart,
darling to the north,
who found a doll one day
and stripped it of its bonnet
and its shoes, the wig of curls,
the promise and the hope,
and left our older sister toyless,
singing servile lullabies and seeking
to slip away without waking
baby to demand more stories
and more years of her life.

Two families under one roof still,
and each day she whispers to indifferent shadows
up long corridors of coastline,
"Love me, love me, too,
I am the older sister."

25

The Ultimate Weapon

Fernando was the bastard boy,
a son unmarried mothers
would be delighted to have born
if they could have their druthers.

The child was illegitimate,
which didn't hold him back;
he loved his Dad so much he left
a doctored almanac.

He handed to historians
a honeyed legacy,
a version deftly edited,
his Dad's biography.

Such filial compassion is
benignly edifying,
a son's gift to his father that
involved a little lying.

He shredded shipboard logs and notes
and mixed a splendid salad,
obscuring flatulence and warts
and later in our ballad

His nephew dissipated all,
despoiled the famous papers
and left us in a soupy fog
regarding Grandpa's capers.

A careless future can conspire
to speckle saint or debtor
unless a relative steps in
and leaves us looking better.

26

The Brother-in-Law

Columbus left a sister
when he headed for the Keys:
Bianchinetta settled for
a man who peddled cheese.

This street-wise hustler dairyman
may well have minced no words
when asked about his relative
while mongering his curds.

"So where's her crazy brother now?"
his customers inquired;
"That boastful, lying horse's ass?
The heavenly-inspired?

"I've never liked the blabbermouth
and may his tongue turn black,
I lent him money for some wine,
He never paid me back.

"The loony thinks he's Ferdinand
the King and puts on airs
pretending he's the cream of cream
while milking millionaires.

"Once sick and tired of cockeyed schemes,
his sister begged him, 'Please,
you ought to find another job.
What's wrong with selling cheese?'"

"And when one day she wakes me up
to cry his ship is wrecked,
I'll shrug and say, 'I told you so,
what else did you expect?'"

27

Rightful Heirs

Those years he struggled to be heard,
the nations chortled, "You're absurd!"

No patrons sought to take a chance
when questioned, "May I have this dance?"
Approached to ante up the cash,
they shied away from acting rash.

Yet once his mission was complete,
he died, all Europe at his feet,
and countries jumped into his bed,
"We mourn our favorite son," they said.

"Hands off him!" cried the Genoese.
"He's one of our celebrities,"
The admiral of Spanish galleons
was claimed by proud-as-punch Italians.

But Corsicans and Portugese
denied the man was Genoese,
and Catalans, Castilians, French
increased the controversy's stench.

Majorcans, Englishmen, and Greeks,
each counterclaimed him in their cliques,
Armenians, Sephardic Jews
laid title when he made the news.

"Colombo, Colón," all explained,
"was what the guy was really named."
Or Collom, Couillons, one of theirs,
while Time, indifferent, yawned, "Who cares?"

A child with vision to disperse
is offspring to the universe.

28

Amerigo Vespucci: The Columbus Corollary

A Florentine, Amerigo,
stood on the shore when Chris returned:
the pickle-maker noted well
what razzmatazz explorers earned
    and thought, "This Spanish conquest pays ya.
    I'm off to get a piece of Asia."

He plotted four expansive trips
though scholars think the record lied
about his journeys to the south,
and when his friend Columbus died,
    Vespucci said, "I'll paraphrase ya,
    And rack in what you left of Asia."

The Spanish throne had cried, "Enough,
no more of pizza in the sky!"
Their competition, Portugal,
which let Columbus flitter by,
    employed him ("It's enough to craze ya,
    Those Spaniards on the loose in Asia.")

He found the Amazon, Brazil,
the Sugar Loaf of Rio Bay,
La Plata, Patagonia,
and back in Portugal, he'd say,
    "What I discovered will amaze ya,
    You know that land? It isn't Asia!"

So here's to you, Amerigo,
who ascertained the tropic scene
was neither Europe nor Far East
but some place somewhere in between.
    Your name still graces that fantasia
    Cartographers once labeled Asia.

HARK! HARK! THE HARQUEBUS!

31

Made in Heaven

They came to the ear of Abraham,
And told him he'd have a son,
They came to stand guard over Israelites,
Protecting the Egypt run.

They came to destroy the Sodomites,
They smote the Assyrian host,
Columbus was tuned to these angels' songs
While cruising along the coast.

Some angels are permanent household help,
Eternally in our hire,
And some crystallize in beholders' eyes
With scabbard and burst of fire.

To those on the islands of parrot wings,
The Spaniards with beads and bells
Were saints from the heavens beyond the earth,
White lightning in caravels.

The natives thought angels had intervened
And met them with dance and song,
Those helmeted cherubim from the sea,
(Boy, talk about being wrong.)

32

Fish and Guests Smell After Three Days

Their visitors, the natives learned,
WEREN'T angels in disguise,
And once the people found this out,
They took to telling lies:

"The shiny stuff lies far away
Plus silver, pearls, and spices,
But better hit the road at dawn
To find your paradises."

When Chris insisted, "Where's the gold?
We want to fill our sacks,"
"Go East, young man," they answered, which
Implied, "Get off our backs!"

"Methinks they would be rid of us,"
Wrote Chris, "they bid us hence,"
Surprised that folks *au naturel*
Would show such common sense.

33

Who Has the Last Cough Now?

To win the natives over,
the Spaniards dangled beads,
brass rings and green and yellow glass,
what every heathen needs.

Along with sorry presents,
the sailors brought disease,
the pox, tubercular bouquets,
kind offerings like these.

Bedazzling folks with mirrors,
the white man made them slaves,
exported them as specimens
to die in Spanish graves.

Before they were extinguished,
deleted from the scene,
the Indians sought sweet revenge,
My Lady Nicotine.

Gratuity for pillage
and booze that made them wacko,
the natives evened up the score:
they hooked us on tobacco.

Where Gold Is Born: A Kiplingesque Caper

"I search for the place where gold is born,"
penned Columbus to queen and king,
"and let's hope other captains don't get to it first,
or I'll have their behinds in a sling.

"Still searching," he wrote, "where gold is born.
"Some natives wear rings in the nose,
and if I can't bring you the ingots you crave,
I'll have to make something of those.

"But should they not willingly part with the loops,
I'll see that their ringlets are snatched,
and if it will please you, I'll throw in the lot,
both nose rings and people attached."

He failed to discern where gold was born;
distinction brought less than peace
and he perished, evicted from golden lands,
where others assumed his lease.

35

Hark! Hark! The Harquebus!

The harquebus is a firearm that
has long been obsolete,
Five hundred years ago the king
conveyed them in his fleet;
The Spaniards knew they'd be of use
when sailing for the East
and fired them freely to impress
and soothe the savage beast.
Hark, hark, the harquebus,
which helped them win the toss
and brought the natives to their knees
more quickly than the cross.

Today Felice, a genteel sort,
enshrines bloodlines and banners,
antiques, old Bibles, coats-of-arms,
and something called "gun manners";
"As children we were taught that guns
deserve respect, affection,
but never in the house," she smiles,
"or aimed in folks' direction."

She adds America and guns
were pals through diverse wrangles;
Felice and I share life and hope
from diametric angles,
And while I hotly emphasize
the boon that gun control is,
my friend appears to look away
no matter what the toll is.
Hark, hark, the harquebus,
a relic from the attic,
ancestor to the handgun and
the semiautomatic.

Hunters and Gatherers

Chiefs, nobles, commoners, and slaves,
Shell gatherers and priests,
Upon such fodder in the heat
The white man's conquest feasts.

The slash-burn jungle poacher carves
A blackened passage rite
To devastate the spindled jaws
That eat the tropic night.

A tribal elegy we sing
Of ecologic toss:
One people's hemispheric gain
Has been another's loss.

What history once viewed as noble
Has repercussions that are global.

37

Ignorance

You do not know, you North Americans,
the swell of Spanish documents
that secured a continent of maize,
manioc, cinchona to salve fever,
woven alpaca, cotton, llama wool,
the Indians at their looms weaving
blankets to hide their fear.

You do not know, you North Americans,
parading *peninsulares* of Old Spain,
the Creole founding fathers,
mestizos, shadings of the jungle,
Araucanians swallowed down rivers of silver,
stirred with crimson and the breath
of languages you never comprehended.

You do not know these colonies at all,
the *audiencias,* the courts that spoke the law,
no fluency have you for Bahia, Rio, Santos,
a land too vast to work, a tiger
by the tail of conquest, Tabatinga
on the Amazon's exultation.

You do not know, you North Americanos,
seesawing gold, a future in the balance,
the land granted in leagues and
conquered in inches, Torsedillas,
what booty was divided, pacts and swords,
battle lines drawn with Amerind blood.

Tribes Found and Lost

Two continents felt the poison dark
of white men, and wild birds wept,
an arc of scarlet plumage spread
in mourning for those who once had crossed
the Bering Sea and fanned downward
till their Asian blood was shed
where *criollos* could spill it into silver chalices.

That they had lived unknown then
and unknown now
should make us cry out
for lost patterns carved on hollow logs,
and the stone knife is gone,
the stripes of red-white hope
painted on shaded faces.

Their rainforest is passing, too,
like the canticle played on the bone flute,
beads broken, chanting voice
stilled with the weakened songbirds.

The Shaman does not conjure up
his predicted ghost, and even our telescopes
focused on rockets weaving baskets
in the universe
do not sight the lost ones
who will not return.

THE ENTROPY OF SUCCESS

41

The Higher Education of Columbus

"I know my astronomy, each rising star."
("You know," creaked the ship, "how unyielding you are.")

"I know bird migrations, know water and cloud."
("You know," sighed the sky, "to be stiff-necked and proud.")

"I know speed and distance, the granules of time."
("You know," puffed the sail, "how you fall when you climb.")

"I know my geography, know every crest."
("You know," called the shore, "how a man is obsessed.")

"I know of betrayal, what envy distills."
("You know," rued the rain, "how your loneliness kills.")

"I know God's solicitude, what Moses had."
("You know," cooed the moon, "what it is to go mad.")

"I know my cartography, know how to chart."
("You know," wept the wind, "how to break your own heart.")

Second Time Around

His subsequent voyage was hardly the equal,
the first a world triumph, the next a mere sequel,
deficient in rhythm, in meter, in rhyme,
the let-down that follows success every time.

No longer anointed by prophets of old,
he shamelessly beat at the bushes for gold
with legions of bureaucrats coiled at his neck
to gauge his ambition and keep it in check.

He, King of the Indies, deserved his own crown,
but jealous inferiors pounded him down,
resented his being the Man of the Year,
"an upstart from somewhere, unknown around here."

It's no easy business to pick up the thread
when men curse your fortune and wish you were dead;
The fort he had founded was blackened and bare,
the men left behind had been massacred there.

But details of mopping up spills were a bore;
he pushed on to places not charted before
and soon he was sure he had Mainland in tow,
(he made his men swear this pronouncement was so.)

Bad luck, though he'd always been tougher than quartz,
he took to his bed in a coma of sorts,
and needing somebody to trust as a tool,
he sent for his brother to manage and rule.

43

His sister, he summoned, relations, a friend,
not power-mad flunkies the Spaniards would send,
who hated his guts, jealous back-biting fops,
and seeking revenge, they uncorked all the stops

to claim there were too many leaders at large,
but not anyone they could say was in charge.
They fumed that the longer he stayed there each day
the country was throwing its money away.

Returning to Spain, though he'd broken no laws,
he met no parades, accolades, or applause;
from those who insulted his honor and mocked,
he made himself scarce, an Explorer Defrocked,

and plugging his ears, he avoided abuse.
They called him a braggart who couldn't produce!

The gold he had promised to bring was a lie.
What good his discovery? What could it buy?
Incompetent foreigner, paranoid, weird,
"The Admiral of the Mosquitoes!" they jeered.

"It costs us a bundle that you may explore,
but you're no great bargain in minding the store."

As Queen Isabella implied more sedately,
"We thank you, but what have you found for us lately?"
And yet when he swore he'd deliver, they'd see,
Kind Providence granted him Trip Number Three.

Running It Into the Ground

As Viceroy of the Indies isles,
He ran a Mom and Pop type store
With worried, calculating smiles
And relatives to guard the stiles.

But he would rather sail than bind
Himself to desk and ledger books,
He let his younger brother mind
Employees who would rob him blind.

Good managers must trust themselves
To keep an eye on jealous help
Lest merchandise depart the shelves
Because of sticky-fingered elves.

MORAL:
Those shops where nepotism veers
Are never short on mutineers.

45

Unlucky Three

If he were to do it once more,
Those voyages after the first,
He'd settle an unfinished score,
Determine the Mainland or burst.

Instead, Trinidad lay due south,
And had he remained on that course,
He'd spit in the Amazon's mouth,
An action his men would endorse.

But who knew a continent lay
Beyond those fresh currents on hand?
He sailed parallel to the bay
And found him a Cloud Cuckoo-Land.

The pinnacle, top of the earth,
The world in the shape of a pear,
Enjoined at the crest of its girth
Four rivers of Paradise there.

When someone obsessed with a dream
Encounters the real but unknown,
A lunatic's riddles may seem
More logical than overblown.

Rebellions like rivers run deep,
Too many were poaching his pearls,
Admitted, he played them too cheap.
Young upstarts with faces like girls.

The monarchs, displeased back in Spain,
Injected new blood with a shrug,
Concluding his governor's reign,
Pulled out their imperial rug.

The Path Downward

The Governor bound him in chains,
Columbus had ceased to be fun,
In spite of bravado and brains,
His downfall had only begun.

They carried him homeward to Spain,
A shocked Isabella and king
Could garner no pleasure or gain
In seeing him dangled on string.

Unshackled, he burst into tears,
"Don't think," they replied, "we forgot,
As Admiral, you have no peers,
A Viceroy with talent you're not."

47

Governor Bobadilla

A Replacement's Lament

What did I do that inflicted his curse?
The king and the queen sent me in as relief
to govern the Indies, the islands, the main,
and I was just doing my job as their Chief:
    I was just doing my job.

Why did that lunatic bear me a gudge?
To bring royal justice to chaos is not
a crime when a foreigner rubs the wrong way
and Spaniards are hung on a scaffold to rot:
    I merely set the men free.

Why did his brother, Diego, resent
my taking their property, papers, and house?
The objects weren't his but the queen's and the king's,
Is that any reason for someone to grouse?
    I had the law on my side.

Why did the Admiral challenge my clout?
It wasn't my power he flouted but Spain's,
compatriots slaughtered, incompetence, fraud,
the sorehead deserved to be shipped back in chains:
    I thought it was a nice touch.

Why did the Monarchs allow his return,
commanding his booty and papers restored,
and for the fourth time give the sorcerer help
when burning should better have been his reward?
    I suspect witchcraft myself.

Why did that devil Colón make the storm
that ruined the journey returning me home
and spared *him,* demolishing twenty-four ships
while five hundred souls (and my own) fed the foam:
    I deserved better than that.

Bon Voyage and Good Riddance

The king sighed, "Enough of this arrogant pest,
We'll fund his Fourth Journey to areas west,
And just as we banished the Hebrew and Moor,
Be rid of this nagging, petitioning boor,

"Including his brothers. I view with dismay
His sailors who dun me, demanding their pay.
I'm weary of quibbling, objections, complaints,
And wild-eyed fanatical prophets and saints.

"Look, even my queen is beginning to wilt
At long-winded pleas and aspersions of guilt,
Of lost compensation, percentages, gain:
Perpetual gratitude, that's his refrain.

"A monarch in Europe has more fish to fry
Than sorting out scuffles in lands gone awry,
I've contracts to ratify, treaties to sign,
My heirs to provide for, and kings to align.

"Colón, you were always affecting a pose,
And why Isabella promotes you, God knows,
Enough of your whining, your privileged right,
Just do me a favor: get out of my sight!"

49

Last Voyage

What? You do not let me, Admiral of the Ocean Sea,
call at the ports of Española?
Damn you, Nicholás de Ovando, you are a goat,
not governor, forbid my anchor at Santo Domingo?

It was I, Cristóbal Colón, day star of the morning,
who discovered Española, and her purpleblue
dimpled waters winking at me in the sun
whispered she was mine, Santo Domingo,
my land, my planet of pleasantness.

Would God forbid my holy lands to me?
He gave me strength to rescue islands
from the ocean's memory while the world
withered with ignorance.
DAMN THEM ALL THE BASTARDS

I have walked naked and barefoot and now you say
I may not set my foot upon my sand?
My voice is as a ghost out of the ground,
each grain is mine, each pearl
holds my vision in its belly.

The flat bluegreen coins of fish
the coral speckled-white medallions
in the stronghold of the sea
black shadows striped with gold not mine
wave me on with their purple lace fins
my Lord of hosts, free me in Jerusalem,
where from the heights I may behold
the earth which is Thy footstool
and inside God, a foreigner no more,
I shall own the world's allegiance
DAMN THEM ALL THE BASTARDS

50

May thorns and briars fall upon my enemies
who are they to tell me where my ships may go?
No one can measure Paradise until he sees it
here where land divides the rivers
the sharks came to tear my flesh
here in the dominion my eyes alone conquered
a diadem of beauty for a queen
I should have offered it to God alone
and named myself prophet and swift messenger
to rule it in His absence
and declare His glory from afar
as sovereigns do who fill their castles
with my despoiled soul

Put not your trust in princes, leviathans,
slant serpents, my earthly Paradise was never theirs,
no no no no no no no the sea
reels to and fro like a drunken Spaniard
and Isaiah cautions me
to where the landfall kneels to kiss my feet
and golden brocade beaches
prostrate themselves and surely
surely surely there are ten days from
here to the River Ganges
where the Great Khan will
love me as a prince
not hireling to Castile and Aragon
and let us say

DAMN THEM DAMN THEM

DAMN THEM ALL THE BASTARDS

51

The Great Khan

And when he reached the Orient,
the mighty Spanish Don
would seek the ruler of that land,
the eminent Great Khan,
the rich-as-ice-cream potentate,
the moneybagged Great Khan.

Aboard the ship one man could speak
Chaldean, Arabic;
he'd translate what the Great Khan spoke
and dazzle him with slick
proposals wrought from Christopher's
hypnotic rhetoric.

For emperors and potentates
would be his cup of tea,
a commoner looks forward to
a spot of monarchy;
it beckons like an opiate
and blurs the pedigree.

He never found the Orient,
that mighty Spanish Don,
and we shall also seek in vain
the ghost phenomenon,
pursuit of boundless opulence,
the slippery Great Khan

the ultimate Great Con.

52

After the Fact

Bartolomé de Las Casas

The journals of Columbus,
The original destroyed,
Were salvaged by a bishop named Las Casas,
Who repaired the faulty passages
As creaky as a ship
And redid them for the educated masses.

It's the bishop's altered version
We depend on to this day
Though he erred, transcribing "league" instead of "mile,"
And he mixed up his directions:
East and west were interchanged,
But he wowed the public with his writing style.

He improved upon the Spanish,
Offered clarity it lacked,
And abridged the cadence and the epithet,
And although we're told he garbled
Certain areas of fact,
After all these years, be glad what you can get.

53

Caribbean Mutiny

The cruise ship was a silver stitch
upon a fractured sea;
I wakened weary of the waves,
the daquiris and me.

Beneath my cabin door a note
was thrust, a ghostly folder,
I brushed away the mist and found
Columbus at my shoulder.

"No travel agent promised *you,"*
I sought the steward's bell
but stopped, detained by sunken eyes
encased in ancient hell.

"You want my younger self," he snarled,
"ambitious, full of beans?"
And from the sea bed seeped a prince
to dazzle kings and queens.

Behind, a young cartographer,
destroying maps he drew,
a dreamer and a pragmatist,
a baptized soul, a Jew.

A doting father floated through
that bloodless coterie
and flanked by fog, the Admiral
who tacked the Ocean Sea.

The stately Renaissance man bowed;
the mystic with clay feet,
the zealot and the scoundrel shared
a boundless winding sheet.

54

The hangman viceroy with his noose,
a braggart, an imposter,
an Aaron and his golden calf
dropped in to sign the roster.

My cabin, straining at the walls,
a Lilliput of arks,
recalled that comic stateroom scene
that ruffled Groucho Marx.

"Ha! Two can play this game!" I shrieked,
and summoned all *my* selves,
who clogged the locker, ceiling, floors,
the medicine chest shelves.

The hundred passengers I am
engaged his schizoid band;
like Jacob and the angel we
did combat hand to hand.

Outnumbered, I jumped overboard,
Columbus to my ears,
my earthly baggage anchored down
with phantom souvenirs.

His apparition haunts me still,
a fitful residue,
which gives no other choice but this:
to foist him off on *you.*

THE BIBLE BUFF

57

Apocryphal Story

Old Esdras borrowed heavily,
was Hebrew subsidized,
He paralleled the Scriptures
which he blithely plagiarized.

He featured Adam, Abraham,
and Noah's cloudburst fame,
and Moses got a plug or two
on how he played the game.

Isaiah, Jeremiah's vibes
are quoted in the script,
a tidal wave of prophecy
in which Columbus dipped.

The Admiral sought passages
to spur his voyage forth
and learned from the Apocrypha
of land mass south and north.

He drew his inspiration from
both Ptolemy and Polo
but claimed the Book of Esdras most
had galvanized his solo.

Columbus owed the man a world
and said so, to his credit,
Our thanks to Esdras and his book
(Most people haven't read it.)

Prophetic Paths

He used the Scriptures, seeking paths,
An angel on his shoulder,
And looked for signpost testaments,
The New one and the Older.

He dropped astronomy and maps
That other men designed,
And swore the prophets of the Book
Had kept his jaunt in mind.

He led the men as Moses had,
And sensed a mighty Hand
Had parted seas and sent the wind
To woo his cranky band.

59

A Political Truth

When Moses was a politician
back in Sinai land,
he had his share of party conflict,
managing his band.

His public speaking didn't sparkle,
neither did his clothes;
his economic program wavered,
making daily foes.

The people hooted at his platform,
those who chose to laugh
included his resentful siblings
and their golden calf.

When Moses won as politician,
strong support was lacking,
the single feather in his cap
was Superhuman backing.

That's how Columbus saw his lot;
the troops were less than frantic,
but Someone higher up took charge
and managed the Atlantic.

Civil Servants of the Bible

Columbus shunned the civil servants
bumbling in Castile
and stiff-necked snubbed the middlemen
who lacked sufficient zeal.

But Moses formed an agency
dispensing regulations;
his interoffice memos soon
became the Hebrew nation's.

But Joseph down in Egypt,
uncorrupted, without stain,
once did an evenhanded job
of handing out some grain.

But prophets of the Holy Book
were reapers and were sowers
(They're what is known in Washington,
D.C. as whistle-blowers).

The Admiral found Bible men
a source of inspiration,
which didn't save him from the sins
of flawed administration.

61

Higher Math

Hebrew writing dwelled on seven,
Days the Lord made earth and heaven,
  It's a numeral much favored down the line,
Seven stars' illumination
Aided New World navigation
  And they kept three ships from sinking in the brine.

In the Bible humble doers,
Servant artisans and hewers,
  Worked for seven years until their bonds were shed,
Seven years Columbus suffered
While his fantasies were buffered
  Seven years he waited for the go-ahead.

Chris, enmeshed within its power,
Brought back seven slaves as dower,
  Indication that he didn't waste his time,
Underneath his gambler's fancy
Waxed a touch of necromancy,
  Indivisible, a seven in its prime.

All you lottery diviners,
Sevenists and forty-niners,
  Scribble down this number for a worthwhile play,
Pay attention, digit lovers,
And this category covers
  Spread sheet statisticians and your CPA.

62

Unprofitable Prophet

(Note: Columbus frequently referred to prophets Isaiah and Jeremiah but may have overlooked Elisha, 9th century B.C. prophet, who succeeded the more famous Elijah, fought idolatry, and appears in legends as a champion of the destitute.)

Let's hear it for form over substance,
for flack work and public relations,
Let's trumpet the prophet Elisha, white knight,
who battled the idols of nations.

The planet has slighted Elisha,
Elijah, his famous professor
partakes of the glory, the Passover wine,
but none for his thirsty successor.

Why don't we hear more of Elisha?
Elijah revealed the direction,
Elisha spent fifty years whacking at Baal,
but wouldn't win any election.

Elijah attends circumcisions,
and sits with the bigtime promoters,
Elisha is out doing work for the poor,
which doesn't impress many voters.

63

Brotherly Breach

(Note: Devoted to his own brothers, Bartolomeo and Diego, Columbus advised his older son Diego to "take care of your brother...nowhere have I found better friends than my brothers." Columbus had learned a thing or two from the Bible and wisely avoided the following familial tensions aired in Genesis.)

"I dreamed a dream," young Joseph bragged,
"The universe I owned,
The sun and moon bowed down to me,"
("Good grief!" his brothers groaned.)

Since Joseph was Pa Jacob's pet,
("My Joe can do no wrong"),
The brothers trapped him in a pit,
And sold him for a song.

No doubt they felt a guilty twinge,
And there'd be hell to pay,
But taking all into account,
They did it anyway.

A lesson in this Bible tale:
Pay heed to children's quibblings,
And never underestimate
The rivalry of siblings.

Connubially Cononical Columbus

All marriages are holy,
some less inclined, some apter;
they parallel the Scriptures,
repeat each verse and chapter.

Some marriages are Proverbs,
staid, wisdom-filled, didactic,
and some, poetic passion,
the Song of Songs, climactic.

Some (see the Book of Daniel)
reveal wild expectation,
or like Ecclesiastes
pile models of frustration.

All marriages are holy,
the losers in this probe
are doomed to Lamentations
or worse, the Book of Job.

Colombo's conscience never
would let him off the hook:
his common law arrangement
was hardly by the Book.

65

The Poem He Never Wrote

1.

I write this letter to your majesties,
Most Catholic monarchs, lions of Castile
And Aragon, this *Libro de las Profecías,*
This book of prophecies, from one who has
Been diving in the sea to find
The pearl of tomorrow. I, your servant,
Don Cristóbal Colón, having been delivered
From my third voyage to the rivers of the
Earthly Paradise, must go forth again,
As God has instructed me through His prophets,
To find the chamber of the Lord in Jerusalem
And rescue it for all who worship Him.
It is my plan to write this book in verse
For I have sipped where unseen springs converge.

Having served Spain as a mariner, I choose
The divinity of the sea over the pettiness of man,
And I have tasted strength
From the islands of the shark
And the fountains of the whale.

My brothers and I, having been arrested
By the scoundrel Francisco de Bobadilla,
Were beaten back to Spain in chains,
Which to this day lay coiled beside my bed
To remind me of man's perfidy.

I have suffered as the Hebrew prophets suffered
Because I knew tomorrow is the golden tide
Embedded in today.

2.

The Lord has counted into my hand His beads:
Astronomy, geometry, arithmetic
Did He bestow on me,
And courage settled on my shoulders
Like the colors of a great title,
And through Him alone I learned to draw the sphere,
And upon it cities, rivers, mountains,
The islands and the harmonies
For which the Lord is praised.

He taught me how to tread the path
To India through His prophets and as
The enemies of tomorrow mock His prophets
So did mine make sport of me, and the Lord
Helped me fight off the jackals
At the court of your majesties, and I was safe
Out upon the water, a newborn child, untouched.

The Lord has called me from the Womb,
From the bowels of my mother he beckoned,
And chose me again to take His word
To the Earthly Paradise and rivers beyond.

Then send me to Jerusalem, I pray,
That I may meet Him on His holy ground
And bring His heart of molten gold
Back to the people who adore His name.

As God knew Moses face to face
So does He know my face, my cheeks, my mouth,
From every night that I stood vigil in the dark
And looked into His shattered holy eye.

WHERE GOLD IS BORN

69

Humble Origins

(Note: In answer to the criticism at court about his common origins, Columbus answered, "After all, David, that wisest of kings, tended sheep and was later made king of Jerusalem, and I am the servant of Him Who raised David to that high state.")

Colombo, you son of a weaver,
whom nobles would envy and cut,
you're labeled an overachiever,
who fled from the wool-carding hut.

Your growing up years are a tangle,
but no one today can surmise
that fleecing the queen was your angle
or pulling the wool over eyes.

Your secrets survive frequent airings,
and charmed by the chaos that mutes you,
I treasure my own humble bearings:
this child of a cobbler salutes you.

70

More Undiscovered Islands

My parent's shoe store stood on Main Street
sixty years ago or more,
planted in the sand, a banner:
immigrants had come ashore.

Not for Spain and Isabella
did they raise their coat of arms,
corridor of pasteboard boxes
in the midst of dairy farms.

They were Europe's blind explorers
blown to land unknown before,
by dead reckoning adventure,
they beguiled the ocean floor.

Not from visions of the prophets
rose their fortress in the wild,
only dreams of Queen Survival
and each dark Depression child.

71

The Yarn of the Bunion Acres

The flagship rig that Columbus sailed,
Round-bellied, unwieldy bark,
Was kissing kin to the boat we were in,
Our slipper-fed Noah's Ark.

No ropes knew we of the sailing sort,
Untutored we braved the breakers,
A shoeworthy store taking leave of the shore,
The humble ship Bunion Acres.

The foresail flaunted its canvas strength
To protect from the sun after dawning,
Where the forecastle lay with cheap shoes on display
Under the orange and green awning.

The keel as short as the boards were worn,
The beam was a narrower space,
And the unpainted pine spelled a splintered design,
The deck of a bargain store place.

The wooden shelves rattled like brittle ribs
To bolster the listing hull,
And each pasteboard box gleamed like seagull flocks
In a sixty-watt sky turned dull.

The ship could load eighty tons of shoes
In its shelves and half-earthen hold,
And the coal furnace burned what the feeble rig earned
While the quarterdeck froze with cold.

The Bunion Acres is long since beached,
Even Main Street has called it quits,
For the Interstate brought our safe harbor to naught,
And developers malled it to bits.

72

A 1930-ish Folk Ballad

Anna and John were outsiders,
He worked in the shoemaker's trade;
They settled down next to Don's Market
In a dairy farming town
        No cash, no friends,
        and they could barely make ends
Encounter.

Don Razorback served as their neighbor,
Grocery entrepreneur,
Specialty gouging and gulling,
Crafty rotten produce czar
        Also well-known
        for peddling gristle and bone
Slyly.

Anna and John had been hoodwinked,
No one explained when they bought
That there was no rear access entrance
To their sliver of a shop
        Landlocked and small,
        a crummy hole in the wall
Lemon.

Anna and John had their garbage
Collected each week by the town,
It carted their trash through an alley,
Title held by Razorback,
        Who pledged that they
        would have complete right of way
Through it.

73

The deed in the courthouse confirmed it,
But Razorback harbored a plan:
He'd trample the small fry adjacent,
And create a supermart
It was ordained,
and if the greenhorns complained,
Squash 'em.

Anna and John had four children,
Who lived with them over the shop,
The upstairs hall harbored one window
Looking out on Don's back door,
It wasn't much,
a little sun in their hutch
Darkly.

Razorback dreamed of expansion
And coveted their right of way,
He'd leave them in shadows like mushrooms
And destroy their only breeze:
Options were few,
but from the conqueror's view,
So what?

For he owned a farm and a homestead
Endowed with a wrap-around porch
And acres of woodland and sunshine
For his barren wife to share
He showed no heart,
nor any reason to start
Changing.

Anna cried, "No, nothing doing,
We bought it, the right of way's ours,
America's not the Old Country,
Ain't we just as good as him?
What's fair is fair:
I want him out of my hair
Net."

The immigrants found an attorney,
Who drank dry martinis with Don,
And tore from their guts fifty dollars
For this lawyerly advice:
"Old Don may sue,
That could be costly to you
People."

A Razorback newphew was sheriff,
A Razorback uncle was judge,
His kinfolk had lived in that county
Since old Hector was a pup
Birthright will tell:
When you've an accent as well,
Forget it."

If this were a Frank Capra movie,
The humble would triumph in spades,
But Don pulled his strings with the neighbors
And blocked windows on all sides
He had no right
to rig the lopsided fight
But did.

Anna and John were outsiders:
Columbus was foreign like them,
The nobles made fun of his accent,
And they stole his right of way:
Power is graphed
in tems of who gets the shaft
Lastly.

75

The Statue Speaks Again

Give me your tired, your poor (she said)
and do not fear abuse,
the new blood feeds my arteries,
I put it to good use.

Give me Korean grocery stores,
your busboy Vietnamese,
your Haitians, Cubans, wrenching free;
my heart is primed with these.

You brought me your European dregs,
rejected and despised,
and soon they mainstreamed in my blood,
a land revitalized.

Give me illegals on the shore,
who keep my lamp ignited,
for they belong like all of you
who came here uninvited.

July 4

No things in life stay constant,
we change at every sitting,
years wear us with corrosion,
time eats us with its pitting.

We thrive on pyrotechnics
that do not last the night,
supplying generations
a fragile candlelight.

Such tapers keep tradition
from ever wearing thin,
as timeless as the summer
we let our freedom in.

77

Thoroughbreds

In the grade school of the shoemaker's girl
reigned two young captains from Castile:
Wilton and Clarence ** Clarence and Wilton,
and Arethusa Perdu Chardwick was the teacher,
full of love for those two princelings
even when they flipped their spitballs
at her shingled shave-necked skull,
pushed and shoved and let her down
(they always let her down) but they had
bloodlines, grace and glory like the
Tootsie Roll tinted horses grazing on
patrician bluegrass land their Hunt Club
people owned for eons of teas and cocktail
parties to which Arethusa Perdu Chardwick
was never invited, and even when they burped
she laughed like Irene Dunne and teased,
"Those two little monkeys of the Amazon,"
Wilton and Clarence ** Clarence and Wilton.

Arethusa Perdu Chardwick found no joy
in me even though I did my lessons, never
pushed in line and never let her down like
Wilton and Clarence ** Clarence and Wilton.
She said I walked too loudly.

My Pop had hammered on my heels steel taps,
clickety clack Shirley Temple impact,
but they deafened Arethusa Perdu Chardwick,
distant cousin to the money, oh so near
and yet so far, squandering spinsterhood
in one half of a rented clapboard mildewed
putty bungalow, hollyhock hidden, weeping
for a royal summons to ride to the hounds
through the silver spoon paved courtyard of
Wilton and Clarence ** Clarence and Wilton.

So once I wrote a composition all about
two little monkeys of the Amazon,
two darling little monkeys, by the name of
Wilton and Clarence ** Clarence and Wilton
who misbehaved, the little devils, and
I handed it to Arethusa Perdu Chardwick who
laughed and laughed who loved it adored it,
and read it to the whole class out loud and
everyone teased, "Those little monkeys
of the Amazon," and turned around, the
towheads twisted like golden jar tops
to look at you-know-who (not me) and I
thought goody gumdrops, I made her laugh
and now she'll love me as much as she does
those two sons of bitches
Wilton and Clarence ** Clarence and Wilton
but the next day she yelled at me:
I walked too loudly
(so much for slanting your material).

And now fifty years later I call to you
Wilton and Clarence ** Clarence and Wilton,
across your crisp white cracker fences,
your rolling bluegrass national velvet
sold out to McDonald's and Penney's and my voice
hits the Security Officer's silver badge
and richochets from Kinney's to Roy Rogers
while rubbertread shoes pad around
the mall on concrete mornings
with the other Senior Citizens round and
round the mall so we can be physically
fit when the pollution knocks us flat
and I say, where are you now you
snotty bastards curdled up in your
capital gains, do you ever think
deep poems about Arethusa Perdu Chardwick?

Fat chance

79

The Visit

You visit your old neighborhood,
whose residents have shifted;
drained doorways tilt like silent shells
from which the sea has drifted.

You marvel at Time's substitutes,
upheaval of the seating,
a foreign placard, script unknown,
an alien deleting.

You pause in urban pilgrimage,
a native disconnected,
your windows sealed, your car door locked,
your innocence protected.

The world around you honks its horn
and pumps accelerator;
it races on, impervious
to who came first or later.

Another Lady of the Club

Maybe when I'm eighty
and the wind is blowing right,
and the publishers are bolder
than a hooker in the night,

you will find this flotsam barrel
on a gray sargasso sea,
brave Columbus of mosquitoes,
jetsam serendipity,

and one reader (with hosannas)
will redeem me from the hacks
and proclaim me "just discovered":
Grandma Moses, Nellie Sachs.

81

El Escritorio

(Dedicated to an antique desk found in the Christopher Columbus Memorial Chapel, Boalsburg, Pennsylvania. A member of the Boal family married into the clan of the Admiral and inherited relics later brought to the United States from the ancestral Colón family castle in Spain.)

If this was the stone underpinning your trip,
If this bore the parchment of your log,
If this was the lecturn of your lies,
Your ambo of petulant authorship

Then why is it catching the northern light,
Landlocked in a rural geography,
Vast leagues from the oceans that heaved you on,
Drydocked in a message you didn't write?

The tourist can crumple the disbelief
That wood you have touched would be hers to see,
The pulpit you used would outlast the foam,
That risk be reduced to a blackened reef.

This skeleton blown by a hurricane
Of circumstance stronger than prophecy
Attests to the wayfaring spirit of mind
In mid-Pennsylvania as well as Spain.

Dim Galaxies

Beyond the constellation Bootes,
The Herdsman tending stellar sheep,
There we'll call, "Tierra! Tierra!"
In the bubble planet's keep.

Indissoluble, the future
Irrigates Castilian dust
As our century of toddling
Holds a universe in trust.

We shall trace the soul of patterns,
Sense the light-years of the blind
Till discovered tricks of matter
Free the Mystery confined.

Come then, brighten splendid rockets:
Stars will speak and heroes pass
Into Time's own freedom marrow,
Into poetry's crevasse.

83

To 2092: Ahoy!

You curators in twenty ninety-two
may look back on these verses and construe
a time more primitive than we bewail
five hundred years ago when Spain set sail.

Those cartoon characters, you'll say of us:
those lords of wormy caravels
ignored the implications of their legacy
and could not see beyond technology

as laughable as his who was obsessed
by swallowing the East, digesting West.
The years don't bring the wisdom that they should,
plutonium unfriendlier than wood.

Still, hopeful as an angel in a dream,
we radio this penetrating beam
across the future, coiled like seaman's rope,
entangled in the category Hope:

Your century, we pray, be better reckoned,
(and if not yours, perhaps the twenty-second).

Epilogue: Time and America

1.

Our ledger of America
the past five hundred years
reflects a certain deficit,
perception in arrears
    of Old Inhabitants who lived
    before Europa came
    and managed daily on their own
    a self-sufficient game.

High cultures, lofty pyramids,
as many dialects
as rainbow birds or jeweled plants,
our forest architects.
    The Mayas spoke their poetry,
    the Incas weren't remiss
    nor were those Aztec epic bards
    to whom we wave a kiss.
En masse the hemispheric tribes
maintained a steady pace
not knowing that it spelled the last
free moments of their race.

2.

Columbus, born of Latin Time,
knew chronic late beginnings,
appointments melting in the sun,
lost halfway through the innings.
    His dream was put on hold for years,
    petitions and appeals
    were left to gather Spanish moss,
    a salesman cooling heels.

The Europeans heralded
the headiness of winning,
through years of Spanish rise and fall,
the English underpinning.
    Our shaman's amulet produced
    conviction, greed, and will;
    our rashness rankled Europe's calm
    and makes them edgy still.

The sea floor cradles Spanish gold,
Queen Isabella's gains,
and Time will not respect our ship
much more than it did Spain's.
    Columbus got the best of Time
    beyond the ocean masses,
    with continents his monument
    he winks at hour glasses.

3.

The where we're coming from is gone,
a tortoise shell we're shedding;
it helps to probe five hundred years
to point to where we're heading.
    And once we learn to read the past,
    our children will not lag
    though challenged by a changing tide:
    resilience be their flag.

For they will find a power
that will lavishly supply
archipeligoes of answers:
what we're looking for and why.